This book, "**Startup Essentials: Launching Your Business Legally & Effectively**," is dedicated to all of those who have journeyed alongside me in the realm of entrepreneurship, and to those who have imparted invaluable lessons in both business and life.

To my former colleagues, business associates, and dear friends – your presence and wisdom have significantly shaped my entrepreneurial path. Each interaction has been a stepping stone towards growth and success.

But above all, I extend my deepest gratitude to my family.

To my parents, Linda and Jerry Craig, and to my sisters, Beth, Jackie, and Kellie – your unwavering support and encouragement have been the bedrock of my journey.

To my mom, in particular, your boundless love and steadfast presence have been my guiding light through every challenge and triumph. Your resilience and determination have been an endless source of inspiration.

No mountain too high, no hill too steep – together, we have overcome obstacles and forged ahead.

This book is a tribute to your love, support, and unwavering belief in me.

For all the lessons learned, the encouragement given, and the love shared – this is for you.

With deepest gratitude and love,

© 2024 Clifford Marketing. All rights reserved.

TABLE OF CONTENTS

 # INTRODUCTION

Welcome to **"Startup Essentials: Launching Your Business Legally and Effectively,"** your comprehensive guide to navigating the exciting yet intricate process of establishing your own business.

Whether you're venturing into the dynamic world of digital marketing, affiliate marketing, or any other industry, this book is designed to equip you with the foundational knowledge required to set up your business on solid legal and administrative grounds.

Embarking on a business journey is more than just an expression of your entrepreneurial spirit; it's a commitment to transforming your innovative ideas into a structured, legally recognized entity that can operate, grow, and thrive in today's competitive marketplace.

While the allure of launching a startup is undeniable, the path to success involves critical steps that must be meticulously planned and executed.

This includes choosing a suitable business name, deciding on the right structure, registering your entity, understanding tax obligations, and establishing a strong online presence.

One of the first decisions you'll face is whether to operate under your personal name or to establish a separate business identity. While using your own name might seem like the simplest route, there are compelling reasons to create a distinct business entity.

© 2024 Clifford Marketing. All rights reserved.

A formal business structure, such as a Limited Liability Company (LLC) or corporation, can offer invaluable benefits, including liability protection, enhanced credibility, potential tax advantages, and a clear separation between your personal and business finances. Moreover, a unique business name and identity can significantly impact your brand's marketability and long-term growth potential.

In this book, we delve into the essentials of starting your business, focusing specifically on the legal and administrative filings necessary to turn your vision into reality. We'll guide you through each step, from selecting and registering your business name to understanding your tax obligations with the IRS, and from setting up your online presence to preparing to accept payments for your digital products or services. Our goal is to make these processes as straightforward and accessible as possible, especially for those who may have never navigated them before.

By the end of this book, you will have a clear roadmap for legally launching your business, equipped with the knowledge to make informed decisions that lay the groundwork for your future success. Whether you're aiming to become a leader in digital marketing, affiliate marketing, or any other field, **"Startup Essentials: Launching Your Business Legally and Effectively"** is your first step towards achieving your entrepreneurial dreams.

Let's embark on this journey together, transforming your passion into a thriving business that's built to last.

© 2024 Clifford Marketing. All rights reserved.

CHAPTER 1

NAMING YOUR BUSINESS

The journey of starting your own business begins with a fundamental yet impactful decision: choosing a name. Your business name is more than just a label; it's the first impression you make on potential customers and a reflection of your brand's identity and values. It sets the tone for how clients perceive your business and can influence everything from brand recognition to your marketing efforts.

This chapter will guide you through the process of naming your business, differentiating between a legal business name and a Doing Business As (DBA) name, checking name availability, and registering your chosen name.

Business Name vs. Doing Business As (DBA)

Legal Business Name:

Your legal business name is the official name of the person or entity that owns the business. If you're the sole proprietor, the legal name is your full name. For partnerships, the legal names are the names of the partners. For LLCs and corporations, the legal name is the one registered with the state government.

Doing Business As (DBA): A DBA, also known as a trade name, fictitious name, or assumed name, allows you to conduct business under a name other than your legal business name. For example, if John Smith runs a digital marketing firm named "Innovative Marketing Solutions" as a sole proprietor, "John Smith" is the legal business name, but he can operate under "Innovative Marketing Solutions" by registering a DBA.

© 2024 Clifford Marketing. All rights reserved.

Tips for Choosing a Business Name

1. **Reflect Your Brand**: Choose a name that reflects the essence of your brand and what you offer. It should resonate with your target audience and give them an idea of what to expect from your business.
2. **Keep It Simple**: Your business name should be easy to spell, pronounce, and remember. A complicated name can hinder your marketing efforts and make it difficult for customers to find you.
3. **Be Unique**: Ensure your name stands out from competitors and captures attention. Avoid names too similar to existing businesses, especially within your industry.
4. **Future-proof Your Name**: Pick a name that is flexible enough to accommodate future growth. Avoid overly specific names that could limit your business's evolution.
5. **Consider Online Presence**: Check the availability of your desired business name as a domain name for your website. Consistency between your business name and domain name is crucial for building a strong online presence.

Checking Name Availability

Before you settle on a name, you need to ensure it's not already in use or trademarked by another company. Use the following steps to check name availability:

1. **Secretary of State's Website**: Most states have an online database where you can search for business names registered in the state.
2. **Trademark Search**: Perform a search on the United States Patent and Trademark Office (USPTO) website to ensure your name isn't federally trademarked.
3. **Domain Name Search**: Use domain registration websites to check if your desired business name is available as a domain name.

© 2024 Clifford Marketing. All rights reserved.

Registering Your Business Name

Once you've chosen an available name, the next step is to make it officially yours by registering it with the appropriate authorities:

- **For Sole Proprietors and Partnerships**: If you're using a DBA, register it with your county clerk's office or the state government, depending on your state's requirements.

- **For LLCs and Corporations**: When you file your formation documents with the state (e.g., Articles of Organization for an LLC), your business name will be automatically registered.

- **Trademark Registration**: Consider registering your business name as a trademark to protect your brand on a national level. This process involves filing an application with the USPTO.

Choosing and registering your business name is a critical step in establishing your brand and legal presence. Take your time to select a name that accurately represents your business and will support your long-term goals.

With your name secured, you can move forward confidently in building your business's identity and reputation.

© 2024 Clifford Marketing. All rights reserved.

CHAPTER 2

SETTING UP YOUR BUSINESS STRUCTURE

Choosing the right business structure is a critical decision that affects your company's legal liabilities, tax obligations, and ability to grow and raise capital.

This chapter will help you understand the different types of business structures available and guide you through the process of selecting and setting up the one that best fits your digital or affiliate marketing business.

Overview of Business Structures

Understanding the basic types of business structures is essential for making an informed decision. Here's a brief overview of the most common forms:

- **Sole Proprietorship**: This is the simplest form of business, where one individual owns and operates the business. It doesn't require formal registration, but it offers no personal liability protection.

- **Partnership**: A business owned by two or more people. Partnerships can be simple to establish and offer more resources and ideas, but partners share liability for business debts.

- **Limited Liability Company (LLC)**: Combining the simplicity of a sole proprietorship or partnership with the liability protection of a corporation, an LLC is often ideal for many small to medium-sized businesses. Profits and losses can pass through to your personal income without facing corporate taxes.

© 2024 Clifford Marketing. All rights reserved.

- **Corporation (C Corp or S Corp)**: Corporations offer the strongest protection from personal liability but are more complex and costly to set up. They are subject to corporate income tax. S Corps offer pass-through taxation but with restrictions on the number and type of shareholders.

Choosing Your Business Structure

When selecting a structure for your digital or affiliate marketing business, consider the following:

- **Liability Protection**: How important is it to separate your personal assets from your business liabilities? An LLC or corporation provides this separation.

- **Taxation**: Consider how different structures will affect your taxes. Sole proprietorships, partnerships, and S Corps offer pass-through taxation, while C Corps are taxed as separate entities.

- **Flexibility and Future Needs**: Think about your business's growth potential and whether you might seek investors, which might make a corporation more appealing.

- **Complexity and Cost**: Weigh the complexity and cost of forming and maintaining the entity. Sole proprietorships and partnerships are simpler, whereas LLCs and corporations require more paperwork and fees.

© 2024 Clifford Marketing. All rights reserved.

Filing with the Secretary of State

For LLCs and corporations, you'll need to file specific documents with your state's Secretary of State office. Here's how to proceed:

- **Choose a Business Name**: Ensure your chosen name is available and complies with state requirements.

- **Prepare and File Formation Documents**: For an LLC, file Articles of Organization. For a corporation, file Articles of Incorporation. These documents typically require basic information about your business, such as its name, principal address, and the names of its owners or directors.

- **Pay the Filing Fee**: Fees vary by state and can range from under $100 to several hundred dollars.

- **Draft an Operating Agreement or Bylaws**: Though not always required, creating an operating agreement (LLC) or bylaws (corporation) is best practice. These documents outline the management structure and operating procedures of your business.

- **Obtain Any Necessary Licenses and Permits**: Depending on your business type and location, you may need additional licenses and permits to operate legally.

© 2024 Clifford Marketing. All rights reserved.

Additional Considerations

- **Registered Agent**: LLCs and corporations are required to have a registered agent—a person or company authorized to receive legal documents on behalf of your business.

- **Annual Reports and Fees**: Many states require LLCs and corporations to file annual reports and pay ongoing fees.

- **Tax Registrations**: You may need to register for state and federal taxes, depending on your chosen structure.

Choosing the right business structure sets the foundation for your company's legal and financial framework. It's a decision that influences your day-to-day operations, tax obligations, and capacity to shield yourself from personal liability.

For digital and affiliate marketers, an LLC often provides the right balance of simplicity and protection, but your specific circumstances and future plans should guide your choice.

Once your structure is established, you'll be well on your way to building a successful business within the legal bounds of your jurisdiction.

© 2024 Clifford Marketing. All rights reserved.

CHAPTER 3

TAX REGISTRATIONS & IRS FILINGS

Navigating tax registrations and IRS filings is a crucial step in establishing your business. It ensures compliance with tax laws and sets up your business for financial management.

This chapter will guide you through obtaining your Employer Identification Number (EIN), understanding state tax obligations, and getting familiar with the tax responsibilities that come with your chosen business structure.

Obtaining an Employer Identification Number (EIN)

An EIN, also known as a Federal Tax Identification Number, is used to identify a business entity for tax purposes. It's necessary for hiring employees, opening a business bank account, and filing tax returns.

- **Who Needs an EIN?**: While sole proprietors without employees can use their Social Security Number, obtaining an EIN is recommended for privacy and professionalism. All other business structures (LLC, partnerships, corporations) require an EIN.

- **How to Obtain an EIN**: You can apply for an EIN through the IRS website, by mail, fax, or phone. The online application process is straightforward and provides an EIN immediately upon completion.

- **Application Details**: Be prepared to provide information about your business, including the legal name, address, and the Social Security Number or previous EIN of the principal officer or owner.

© 2024 Clifford Marketing. All rights reserved.

State Tax Registrations

In addition to federal taxes, your business may be subject to various state taxes, depending on where it operates and the nature of its activities.

- **Sales Tax**: If you're selling goods or certain services, you might need to collect and remit sales tax. Registration for a sales tax permit is usually done through your state's department of revenue or taxation.

- **Employer Taxes**: If you have employees, you'll need to register for state employer taxes, which may include unemployment insurance tax and state income tax withholding.

- **Other State Taxes**: Depending on your business and location, you may face additional taxes, such as franchise taxes for LLCs and corporations.

Understanding Your Tax Obligations

Your business structure affects your federal tax obligations, primarily how your business income is taxed.

- **Sole Proprietorships and Partnerships**: Income and losses from the business are "passed through" to the owners' personal tax returns, and they pay personal income tax on business profits.

- **LLCs**: By default, LLCs are treated as pass-through entities for tax purposes, similar to sole proprietorships or partnerships. However, an LLC can elect to be taxed as a corporation.

© 2024 Clifford Marketing. All rights reserved.

- **Corporations (C Corps)**: C Corps are taxed as separate entities. They file a corporate tax return and pay taxes at the corporate tax rate. Dividends paid to shareholders are taxed again on the individual's tax return.

- **S Corporations**: S Corps are pass-through entities, but they avoid the double taxation of C Corps. Profits and losses are passed through to shareholders' personal tax returns.

Keeping Records and Reporting

Accurate record-keeping is essential for managing your tax obligations. Maintain detailed records of income, expenses, and any tax payments or filings.

- **Annual Tax Returns**: All businesses must file an annual income tax return. The form varies depending on your business structure (Schedule C for sole proprietors, Form 1065 for partnerships, Form 1120 for C Corps, and Form 1120S for S Corps).

- **Quarterly Estimated Taxes**: If you expect to owe tax of $1,000 or more when your return is filed, you should make quarterly estimated tax payments.

© 2024 Clifford Marketing. All rights reserved.

Seeking Professional Help

Considering the complexity of tax laws and the potential consequences of errors, consulting with a tax professional or accountant is highly recommended. They can provide personalized advice and ensure your business meets all its tax obligations.

Understanding and managing your tax registrations and IRS filings are fundamental to running a successful business. By taking the time to register for the necessary taxes and understand your obligations, you set your business on the path to compliance and financial health.

Whether you're a digital marketer, affiliate marketer, or entrepreneur in another field, tackling your tax responsibilities head-on is a crucial step in building a solid business foundation.

© 2024 Clifford Marketing. All rights reserved.

CHAPTER 4

SETTING UP YOUR ONLINE PRESENCE

In today's digital age, establishing a robust online presence is essential for the success of any business, especially for those in digital and affiliate marketing.

This chapter will guide you through the crucial steps of registering your domain name, creating a professional website, and setting up business email accounts.

These foundational elements not only legitimize your business in the eyes of customers and partners but also serve as critical tools for marketing, communication, and sales.

Registering Your Domain Name

Your domain name is your online address; it's how customers find you on the internet. Choosing the right domain name is as important as naming your business—it should be memorable, easy to spell, and reflect your brand.

- **Choosing a Domain Name**: Aim for a domain name that matches or closely resembles your business name. Use keywords related to your industry to improve search engine visibility. Avoid numbers and hyphens, as they can confuse potential visitors.

- **Domain Registration**: Once you've chosen a domain name, you need to register it through a domain registrar. Companies like GoDaddy, Namecheap, and Google Domains offer domain registration services. During registration, you can also decide how long you wish to register the domain for, typically ranging from one to ten years, with the option to renew.

© 2024 Clifford Marketing. All rights reserved.

- **Privacy Protection**: Consider adding privacy protection to your domain registration. This service hides your personal information from the public WHOIS database, protecting you from spam and unsolicited contacts.

Creating a Professional Website

Your website is often the first point of contact between your business and potential customers. It should be visually appealing, easy to navigate, and optimized for search engines.

- **Website Building Platforms**: For those without web development skills, platforms like WordPress, Squarespace, and Wix offer user-friendly tools to create professional-looking websites. These platforms provide templates, drag-and-drop editors, and integrations with various business tools.

- **Content Management**: Ensure your website content accurately represents your business and offerings. Include clear descriptions of your services or products, about us page, contact information, and calls to action encouraging visitors to engage with your business.

- **SEO Basics**: Optimize your website for search engines to improve visibility. Use relevant keywords, create quality content regularly, and ensure your site is mobile-friendly. Also, set up Google Analytics to track website performance and visitor behavior.

© 2024 Clifford Marketing. All rights reserved.

Setting Up Professional Email Accounts

A professional email address that uses your domain name (e.g., name@yourdomain.com) enhances your credibility and brand identity.

- **Email Hosting**: Many domain registrars offer email hosting services, allowing you to create custom email addresses. Alternatively, services like Google Workspace and Microsoft 365 provide business email hosting along with access to productivity tools.

- **Creating Email Addresses**: Create email addresses for different purposes (e.g., contact@yourdomain.com, support@yourdomain.com) to organize communications and present a professional image.

- **Email Signatures**: Use professional email signatures that include your contact information, website, and social media links. This not only looks professional but also makes it easy for recipients to find more information about your business.

Conclusion

Setting up your online presence is a pivotal step in launching your business. A thoughtfully chosen domain name, a well-designed website, and professional email addresses lay the groundwork for your digital marketing efforts and help establish your brand in the digital marketplace.

By following these steps, you'll create a strong foundation that supports the growth and success of your business in the digital and affiliate marketing arenas.

© 2024 Clifford Marketing. All rights reserved.

CHAPTER 5

SOCIAL MEDIA & DIGITAL PRESENCE

Social media and a broader digital presence are indispensable tools for businesses in the digital era, especially for those in digital and affiliate marketing.

This chapter dives into strategies for choosing the right social media platforms, setting up and managing accounts, and developing a content strategy that aligns with your business goals.

Establishing a strong digital presence extends beyond social media to include other digital channels like blogs, podcasts, and email newsletters, enhancing your visibility and engagement with your target audience.

Choosing the Right Platforms

Not all social media platforms will be relevant to your business. Selecting the right ones depends on your target audience, the nature of your products or services, and where your potential customers are most active.

- **Research Your Audience**: Understand the demographics of your target audience and match these with the platforms they use most. For instance, LinkedIn is ideal for B2B businesses, while Instagram and TikTok are better suited for reaching younger, B2C audiences.

- **Consider Your Content Type**: Visual products or services are well showcased on platforms like Instagram and Pinterest. In contrast, Twitter and Facebook are great for community engagement and sharing updates or articles.

© 2024 Clifford Marketing. All rights reserved.

Once you've identified the most suitable platforms for your business, the next step is to set up your accounts. Consistency across platforms is key to brand recognition.

- **Use a Consistent Name**: Ideally, your social media handles should match your business name. If your preferred name is taken, find a close variation that remains recognizable to your brand.
- **Complete Your Profiles**: Fill in all available fields with up-to-date information about your business, including your website, a brief bio, and contact details. Use high-quality logos and images that align with your branding.
- **Verification**: For added credibility, consider verifying your accounts, if possible. Verified accounts are marked with a blue checkmark, indicating authenticity.

Developing a Content Strategy

A well-thought-out content strategy helps in engaging your audience, building brand awareness, and driving traffic to your website.

- **Set Clear Goals**: Whether it's increasing brand awareness, driving sales, or engaging with customers, your goals should guide your content strategy.
- **Understand Your Audience**: Create content that resonates with your audience's interests, needs, and challenges. Use social media insights and analytics to understand what content performs best.
- **Content Calendar**: Plan your content in advance with a content calendar. This helps in maintaining a consistent posting schedule and ensures a good mix of content types (e.g., posts, videos, live sessions).
- **Engagement**: Social media is not just about broadcasting your messages; it's about engaging with your audience. Respond to comments, participate in conversations, and encourage user-generated content.

© 2024 Clifford Marketing. All rights reserved.

Beyond social media, consider other channels to broaden your digital footprint:

- **Blogging**: A blog can drive traffic to your website, improve your search engine rankings, and establish your authority in your industry.

- **Email Newsletters**: Keep your audience updated with regular newsletters featuring valuable content, company news, and exclusive offers.

- **Podcasts or Webinars**: These can be effective ways to reach your audience, share expertise, and engage with customers on a deeper level.

Measuring Success

Track your performance across platforms using analytics tools provided by social media platforms and third-party applications. Metrics such as engagement rates, follower growth, and website traffic from social channels will help you refine your strategy and achieve your business objectives.

Conclusion

Building a robust social media and digital presence is crucial for modern businesses. It allows you to reach and engage with your target audience, strengthen your brand, and achieve your marketing goals.

By carefully selecting platforms, creating consistent and engaging content, and measuring your success, you can leverage the power of digital channels to grow your business in the competitive digital marketing and affiliate marketing landscapes.

© 2024 Clifford Marketing. All rights reserved.

CHAPTER 6

PREPARING TO ACCEPT PAYMENTS

For any business, especially those in digital and affiliate marketing, setting up a system to accept payments is crucial for operational success.

This chapter will guide you through the essentials of preparing your business to accept payments, including setting up a business bank account, choosing the right payment processors, and understanding the importance of secure payment gateways.

Setting Up a Business Bank Account

A dedicated business bank account is the first step in streamlining your financial operations, ensuring legal compliance, and enhancing your brand's credibility.

When choosing a bank, prioritize one with a strong digital banking interface and minimal fees, and ensure you have the necessary documents like your EIN and business formation papers ready for account setup.

- **Choosing a Bank**: Look for a bank that offers services tailored to small businesses, with low fees and good customer service. Consider both traditional banks and online banking options.

- **Required Documents**: To open a business bank account, you'll typically need your Employer Identification Number (EIN), business formation documents, and ownership agreements. Requirements may vary by bank and business structure.

© 2024 Clifford Marketing. All rights reserved.

- **Account Types**: Decide whether you need a checking account, savings account, or both. A checking account is essential for daily operations, while a savings account can help you manage business savings for taxes or emergencies.

Choosing a Payment Processor

A payment processor facilitates transactions between your business, your customers, and the banks. It's important to choose one that fits your business model, sales volume, and the preferences of your target market.

- **Types of Payment Processors**: There are various payment processors, including merchant account providers (traditional banks) and third-party processors (e.g., PayPal, Stripe). Third-party processors are often easier to set up and more flexible for small businesses.

- **Fees and Contracts**: Compare transaction fees, monthly fees, and any other associated costs. Also, be wary of long-term contracts and early termination fees.

- **Supported Payment Methods**: Ensure the processor supports a wide range of payment methods, including credit cards, debit cards, and digital wallets, to accommodate your customers' preferences.

Leveraging Technology Platforms for Payments and Product Hosting

In addition to traditional payment processors, platforms like Stan Store and Systeme.io offer integrated solutions for digital and affiliate marketers, streamlining the process of accepting payments and hosting digital products.

© 2024 Clifford Marketing. All rights reserved.

Stan Store:

Ideal for creators and marketers looking to sell digital products or subscriptions, Stan Store provides a user-friendly platform for managing your digital storefront. It offers built-in payment processing capabilities, meaning you can sell your products directly without needing a separate payment processor. Key features include customizable product pages, secure file hosting, and automated delivery of digital products upon purchase.

Systeme.io:

A comprehensive tool for online business management, Systeme.io not only facilitates payment processing but also offers features for email marketing, funnel creation, and course hosting. It's an all-in-one platform that allows you to create and sell digital products, manage affiliates, and automate your marketing efforts. With its integrated payment gateway, you can easily set up product pages and accept payments with minimal setup.

Secure Payment Gateways

The payment gateway is the technology that captures and transfers payment data from the customer to the acquirer. It's a critical component of the e-commerce process, ensuring that transactions are securely processed.

© 2024 Clifford Marketing. All rights reserved.

Security Standards: Look for payment gateways that comply with the Payment Card Industry Data Security Standard (PCI DSS). This ensures that your customers' payment information is securely handled and stored.

Integration: The payment gateway should integrate seamlessly with your website and shopping cart software. Many payment processors offer their own gateways, but it's worth checking compatibility.

Customer Experience: The payment process should be smooth and straightforward. A good payment gateway will minimize payment declines and reduce cart abandonment rates by offering features like saved payment information for repeat customers.

Implementing Your Payment System

- **Website Integration**: Work with your web developer to integrate the payment processor and gateway into your website. Ensure that the payment page is branded and provides a seamless checkout experience.

- **Testing**: Before going live, thoroughly test the payment system to ensure that transactions are processed smoothly and securely. Check for any issues with different payment methods and devices.

- **Compliance and Security**: Regularly update your system to comply with security standards and protect against fraud. Consider additional security measures like two-factor authentication and encryption.

© 2024 Clifford Marketing. All rights reserved.

For platforms like Stan Store and Systeme.io, much of the technical heavy lifting is handled by the platform itself, allowing you to focus on customizing your product offerings and optimizing the customer experience.

Ensure that your payment and product delivery systems work seamlessly across all devices and browsers, providing a smooth and secure checkout process for your customers.

Conclusion

By strategically combining traditional payment processing methods with powerful technology platforms like Stan Store and Systeme.io, you can create a robust infrastructure for selling digital products and services.

These platforms not only simplify the payment acceptance process but also provide valuable tools for product hosting, marketing automation, and customer engagement.

As you build and refine your payment and product hosting system, keep your focus on security, user experience, and alignment with your business objectives to foster growth and build lasting customer relationships.

© 2024 Clifford Marketing. All rights reserved.

CONCLUSION

Congratulations on reaching the end of "Startup Essentials: Launching Your Business Legally and Effectively."

By now, you've armed yourself with the crucial knowledge needed to navigate the foundational aspects of starting a business.

From naming your business and choosing the right structure to setting up your online presence and preparing to accept payments, you're now equipped to take your entrepreneurial vision from concept to reality.

Recap of Key Steps

- **Naming Your Business**: Remember the importance of choosing a name that reflects your brand and is easy to remember. Make sure to check for its availability and register it.

- **Setting Up Your Business Structure**: Choose the structure that best suits your needs, considering factors like liability, taxation, and operational complexity. File the necessary documents with your state's Secretary of State.

- **Tax Registrations and IRS Filings**: Obtain your EIN, register for state taxes, and understand your tax obligations to ensure compliance and efficient financial management.

- **Setting Up Your Online Presence**: Secure a domain name, build a professional website, and establish professional email accounts to solidify your digital footprint.

© 2024 Clifford Marketing. All rights reserved.

- **Social Media and Digital Presence**: Select the right platforms for your audience, create consistent and engaging content, and use these channels to b

- **Preparing to Accept Payments**: Open a business bank account, choose a suitable payment processor, and consider platforms like Stan Store and Systeme.io for an integrated approach to selling digital products and services.

Encouragement to Take the First Step

Starting a business can be a daunting journey, but remember, every successful business began with a single step. Don't let the fear of the unknown hold you back. Use the knowledge you've gained here to move forward with confidence. Your entrepreneurial journey is a learning experience, filled with opportunities for growth and success.

Resources for Future Learning

The business world is ever-evolving, and continuous learning is key to staying ahead. Leverage online courses, webinars, and industry blogs to keep up with the latest trends and best practices. Networking with other entrepreneurs and joining relevant online communities can also provide valuable insights and support.

© 2024 Clifford Marketing. All rights reserved.

Additional Resources

To assist you further on your journey, here's a list of essential resources:

Secretary of State Websites

- Every state has its own Secretary of State website where you can find information on business registration, legal requirements, and more. A comprehensive list can be found at National Association of Secretaries of State (NASS).

IRS

- For tax registrations, obtaining an EIN, and understanding federal tax obligations, visit the Internal Revenue Service (IRS) website.

Domain Registrations

- **DreamHost**: https://www.dreamhost.com/

- **GoDaddy**: https://www.godaddy.com/

These platforms offer domain registration services and web hosting solutions to help establish your online presence.

© 2024 Clifford Marketing. All rights reserved.

Social Media Platforms

- **Facebook**: https://www.facebook.com

- **Instagram**: https://www.instagram.com

- **TikTok**: https://www.tiktok.com

- **LinkedIn**: https://www.linkedin.com

- **X / Twitter**: https://www.twitter.com

Each platform offers unique opportunities for building your digital presence and engaging with your audience.

Payment and Product Hosting

- **Stan Store**: For hosting and selling digital products.

- **Systeme.io**: An all-in-one platform for managing your online business.

Embarking on your business journey is an exciting step towards realizing your entrepreneurial dreams. With the right preparation and resources, you can build a successful and sustainable business.

Remember, the path to success is a journey of continuous learning, growth, and adaptation. Best wishes on your entrepreneurial adventure!

© 2024 Clifford Marketing. All rights reserved.

BONUS CHAPTER
REVOLUTIONIZING YOUR BUSINESS WITH CANVA

In the digital age, the visual aspect of your business plays a crucial role in capturing the attention of your audience. Whether it's your website, social media posts, or marketing materials, a strong visual presence can significantly enhance your brand's appeal.

This is where Canva, a powerful yet user-friendly design tool, comes into play. Designed for entrepreneurs, especially those in digital marketing, Canva offers a plethora of features to create stunning visuals without the need for extensive graphic design skills.

This bonus chapter will guide you through what Canva is and how you can leverage its capabilities to revolutionize your business.

What is Canva?

Canva is an online design and publishing tool that democratizes design, making it accessible to people without a graphic design background. With its drag-and-drop interface, thousands of templates, and vast library of images, fonts, and design elements, Canva enables you to create professional-quality graphics, presentations, social media posts, and more. Whether you're designing a logo, a promotional flyer, or social media content, Canva's intuitive platform makes the design process seamless and efficient.

Getting Started with Canva

1. **Sign Up**: First, <u>create a Canva account by signing up on their website</u>. You can start with a free account, which offers a wide range of features, or opt for a Pro account for access to premium templates and design elements.

© 2024 Clifford Marketing. All rights reserved.

2. Explore Templates: Canva offers templates for almost any type of design, from Instagram posts to business presentations. Start by choosing a template that suits your needs, or create a design from scratch if you're feeling adventurous.

3. Customize Your Design: Use Canva's drag-and-drop editor to customize your chosen template. You can change the text, fonts, colors, and images to match your brand's identity. With Canva's Pro version, you can also upload your brand elements, like logos and specific fonts, to keep your designs consistent.

4. Utilize Design Elements: Canva provides a wealth of design elements, including icons, shapes, and stock photos. Use these to enhance your design and make it more engaging.

5. Collaborate and Share: Canva allows you to collaborate with team members by sharing your designs and gathering feedback. Once your design is complete, you can download it in various formats or share it directly from Canva to your social media accounts or website.

How Canva Can Revolutionize Your Digital Marketing Business

- Brand Consistency: With Canva, you can ensure that all your marketing materials, from your website to your social media posts, reflect your brand identity consistently, which is key to building trust and recognition among your audience.

- Engaging Visual Content: Create visually appealing content that captures your audience's attention and communicates your message effectively. Engaging visuals are more likely to be shared, increasing your brand's visibility.

© 2024 Clifford Marketing. All rights reserved.

- **Quick and Cost-Effective**: Canva eliminates the need for expensive design software or hiring a professional designer for every small project. It allows you to quickly create designs in-house, saving both time and money.

- **Social Media Mastery**: Use Canva to design eye-catching social media posts and ads tailored to each platform's recommended dimensions. Consistent, high-quality visuals can significantly increase your social media engagement and follower growth.

- **Marketing Collaterals**: Beyond digital designs, Canva is also great for creating print materials like business cards, flyers, and posters, allowing for a unified brand experience online and offline.

Conclusion

For entrepreneurs in the digital marketing sphere, Canva is an invaluable tool that empowers you to create professional-quality designs with ease.

By incorporating Canva into your business toolkit, you can elevate your brand's visual identity, engage your audience more effectively, and stand out in the competitive digital landscape.

Start exploring Canva today, and unleash the potential of visual content to revolutionize your business.

© 2024 Clifford Marketing. All rights reserved.

ADDITIONAL BONUS CHAPTER
CREATING YOUR BUSINESS PLAN

Introduction

Begin by emphasizing the importance of a business plan for anyone looking to start a business. Explain how it serves as a roadmap, helping entrepreneurs navigate through the early stages of their business, secure funding, and strategically grow. Highlight that this chapter is designed for beginners, aiming to demystify the process of creating a business plan.

Understanding the Purpose of Your Business Plan

Discuss the dual purpose of a business plan: guiding your business operations and convincing investors or lenders of the viability of your business idea. Stress the importance of clarity, accuracy, and realism.

Section 1: Executive Summary

- **What It Is**: An overview of your business and your plan. It includes your business's mission statement, basic information about your company (including ownership and structure), your products or services, and a summary of your future plans.

- **How to Write It**: Write this section last but place it first in your business plan. Keep it concise and engaging. Aim to capture the essence of your business and why it will be successful.

© 2024 Clifford Marketing. All rights reserved.

Section 2: Business Description

- **What It Is**: Detailed information about your business. It explores the problem your business solves, your target market, and the competitive landscape.

- **How to Write It**: Focus on the value your business provides. Conduct market research to present a clear picture of your target audience and how you stand out from competitors.

Section 3: Market Analysis

- **What It Is**: An examination of your industry, market size, expected growth, your target market's characteristics, and trends within the industry.

- **How to Write It**: Use credible sources for your data. Include graphs and charts to illustrate market trends and size. Clearly define your target market and explain your place within the overall market.

Section 4: Organization and Management

- **What It Is**: A breakdown of your business's organizational structure, details about the ownership of the company, profiles of your management team, and the qualifications of your board of directors.

- **How to Write It**: Create an organizational chart to visually present your company's structure. Include brief bios of key team members that highlight their relevant experience and roles in your business.

© 2024 Clifford Marketing. All rights reserved.

Section 5: Products or Services

- **What It Is**: A detailed description of your products or services, including information about the lifecycle, benefits to your customers, and your product's or service's current development stage.

- **How to Write It**: Focus on the benefits and value your product or service brings to customers. If applicable, discuss any research and development activities.

Section 6: Marketing and Sales Strategy

- **What It Is**: Your plan for attracting and retaining customers. This section outlines your marketing strategies, sales tactics, and the overall sales process.

- **How to Write It**: Describe your marketing channels, pricing strategy, sales process, and customer service strategies. Be specific about how you'll measure success.

Section 7: Funding Request

- **For Those Seeking Financing**: An outline of your funding requirements over the next five years, how you intend to use the funds, and possible future financial strategies.

- **How to Write It**: Be clear and specific about the amount of funding you need and offer detailed explanations for how it will be used.

© 2024 Clifford Marketing. All rights reserved.

- **What It Is**: A forecast of your business's financial future, including projected income statements, balance sheets, cash flow statements, and capital expenditure budgets.

- **How to Write It**: Provide realistic projections that reflect your market analysis and funding request. Use charts and graphs to help visualize the data.

Conclusion: The Journey Ahead with Your Business Plan

Creating your business plan is just the beginning of an exciting journey into entrepreneurship. This document is not just a requirement for securing funding or a formal exercise in business development. It is a living, breathing guide that reflects your vision, your goals, and the roadmap to achieve them. As you embark on this journey, remember the following key points to maximize the value of your business plan:

Continuous Improvement

Your business plan should evolve as your business grows and as market conditions change. Regularly review and update your plan to reflect new insights, challenges, and opportunities. This iterative process ensures that your business remains aligned with your strategic objectives and responsive to the external environment.

Strategic Decision-Making

Use your business plan as a decision-making tool. It serves as a benchmark for evaluating the viability of new opportunities and the impact of potential strategic decisions. By referring back to your plan, you can ensure that your business remains on track to achieving its goals and that any deviations are intentional and strategic.

© 2024 Clifford Marketing. All rights reserved.

Communication Tool

Your business plan is a powerful communication tool, not just for potential investors and lenders, but also for your employees, partners, and customers. It articulates your vision, your value proposition, and your strategy for success. Sharing your business plan with key stakeholders can foster alignment, generate buy-in, and build excitement around your business vision.

Learning and Reflection

The process of creating your business plan is as valuable as the final product itself. It compels you to think critically about every aspect of your business, from your value proposition to your financial projections. This deep dive into your business model and market environment is a learning experience that can uncover insights and inspire innovative approaches to challenges.

Foundation for Future Growth

Consider your business plan as the foundation upon which your business will grow. It sets the stage for future expansions, product developments, and market entries. As you reach milestones outlined in your plan, celebrate these achievements and set new goals. Your business plan is a testament to your entrepreneurial journey, from conception to realization and beyond.

In conclusion, "Creating Your Business Plan" is more than an exercise in documentation; it is an essential step in bringing your vision to life. Approach it with enthusiasm and diligence, knowing that this plan is your roadmap to success. It will guide you, challenge you, and support you as you navigate the complexities of starting and growing your business. Remember, the most successful businesses are those that are planned with care and executed with precision. Your business plan is your first step towards achieving that success.

© 2024 Clifford Marketing. All rights reserved.

Recap: Enhancing Your Startup with Canva and a Solid Business Plan

Bonus Chapter 1: Leveraging Canva for Visual Impact

In the digital landscape, visual appeal is paramount. Canva offers a user-friendly platform that empowers entrepreneurs, especially those in digital marketing, to create professional visuals effortlessly. This chapter guides you through Canva's basics, from account setup to design creation, emphasizing its role in achieving brand consistency and engaging content. Canva simplifies visual content creation, making it accessible and cost-effective, thereby revolutionizing your digital marketing strategy.

Bonus Chapter 2: Crafting Your Business Plan

A well-structured business plan is crucial for navigating the early stages of your startup, securing funding, and guiding strategic growth. This chapter outlines the essential components of a business plan, including market analysis, organizational structure, marketing strategies, and financial projections. It underscores the business plan's significance as a roadmap for success and a tool for ongoing improvement and strategic decision-making. Creating a business plan is depicted as a foundational step towards realizing your entrepreneurial vision.

Together, these chapters equip you with the tools to visually and strategically set your startup apart. By combining Canva's visual design capabilities with a comprehensive business plan, you can enhance your brand's appeal and lay a solid foundation for your business's success.

© 2024 Clifford Marketing. All rights reserved.

ABOUT THE AUTHOR

J Craig is an accomplished entrepreneur whose diverse business ventures span from food trucks and lawn care companies to short-term rental businesses, cleaning companies, flipping houses, and the interior design of Airbnb rentals.

With decades of firsthand experience in creating and nurturing businesses from inception to operational success, J has mastered the art of entrepreneurship with a steadfast commitment to legality and ethics.

His entrepreneurial journey has culminated in the founding of a successful digital marketing company, where J dedicates himself to educating others on the potential of making money online. He champions the cause of financial freedom through self-employment, emphasizing the critical importance of conducting business within legal and moral boundaries.

In addition to his digital marketing endeavors, J Craig is the founder of Rental Revenue Revolution: The Ultimate Airbnb Arbitrage Course. This innovative course offers a comprehensive guide to breaking into the Airbnb market through rental arbitrage, a testament to J's expertise and success in the short-term rental industry.

© 2024 Clifford Marketing. All rights reserved.

J is also the author of "Unlocking the Secrets of Airbnb Arbitrage: Your Gateway to Financial Freedom Through Rental Success," an e-book that delves deep into the strategies for achieving success in the Airbnb business model without owning property. This work further establishes J as a knowledgeable and trusted advisor in the realm of rental entrepreneurship.

J's approach to business is not just about achieving financial success; it's about building sustainable, ethical, and legal business models that empower individuals to become successful entrepreneurs.

Through his writings and courses, J Craig offers a roadmap to financial independence, rooted in practical experience and a profound understanding of the business landscape.

His guidance is an invaluable resource for anyone looking to navigate the complexities of starting and running a successful business in today's competitive environment.

His eBook, "Startup Essentials: Launching Your Business Legally and Effectively," encapsulates his philosophy of business: a blend of ambition, legal savvy, and a strong moral compass. With J Craig as a guide, readers are not just learning how to start a business—they're learning how to build a legacy.

© 2024 Clifford Marketing. All rights reserved.

EBOOK FREEBIES:

Turning Passion into Profits

growthwithj.com

Unlocking the Secrets of Airbnb Arbitrage

growthwithj.com/ebookbnb

OPPORTUNITIES:

Rental Revenue Revolution:
The Ultimate Airbnb Arbitrage Course

growthwithj.com/airbnb

Airbnb Course Affiliate

growthwithj.com/affiliate

How to Build Funnels

stan.store/growthwithj

© 2024 Clifford Marketing. All rights reserved.

Pre-Built Squeeze Page Funnel

(Import/Upload into your systeme.io account)

systeme.io/funnel/share/29144994f9023f1f8a4776de07e4aadf6d176f3

Sign up for Systeme.io

systeme.io/?sa=sa01615583907b17308fd4e5386d4a1fcad4ef463e

Build Your Stan Store

join.stan.store/growthwithj

Sign up for Canva

canva.com

Secretary of State Sites

activefilings.com/information/sos-access/

© 2024 Clifford Marketing. All rights reserved.

The End

This is not a get rich quick program nor do we believe in overnight success. We believe in hard work, integrity, and developing skills if you want to earn more financially. As stipulated by law, we cannot and do not make any guarantees about your ability to get results or earn any money with any of our products or services. The average person who buys any "how-to" information gets little to no results. Any references or examples used within the eBook and website are real and documented but are used strictly for example purposes only. Your results will vary and depend on many factors, including but not limited to your background, experience, and work ethic. All business entails risk as well as massive and consistent effort and action. If you're not willing to accept that, please DO NOT PURCHASE ANY PRODUCTS FROM US.

growthwithj.com
© 2024 Clifford Marketing. All rights reserved.

Copyright and Legal Notice

Title: Startup Essentials: Launching Your Business Legally and Effectively
Author: J Craig
ISBN: 9798879975574
Publisher: Clifford Marketing
Year: 2024

All rights reserved. No part of this publication may be reproduced, stored in a retrieval system, or transmitted in any form or by any means, electronic, mechanical, photocopying, recording, or otherwise, without the prior written permission of the author and publisher.

The information contained within this eBook is strictly for educational and informational purposes. While every attempt has been made to verify the information provided in this publication, neither the author nor the publisher assumes any responsibility for errors, omissions, or contrary interpretation of the subject matter herein.

This eBook is not intended as legal or financial advice. The views expressed are those of the author alone, and should not be taken as expert instruction or commands. The reader is encouraged to seek the services of competent professionals in the legal, financial, and marketing fields as deemed necessary.

The author and publisher disclaim any warranties (express or implied), merchantability, or fitness for any particular purpose. The author and publisher shall in no event be held liable to any party for any direct, indirect, punitive, special, incidental, or other consequential damages arising directly or indirectly from any use of this material, which is provided "as is," and without warranties.

As always, the advice of a competent legal, tax, accounting, or other professional should be sought. The author and publisher do not warrant the performance, effectiveness, or applicability of any sites listed or linked to in this eBook.

All trademarks and registered trademarks appearing in this eBook are the property of their respective owners.

Users of this eBook are advised to do their own due diligence when it comes to making business decisions and all information, products, services that have been provided should be independently verified by your own qualified professionals. By reading this document, the reader agrees that under no circumstances is Clifford Marketing responsible for any losses, direct or indirect, that are incurred as a result of the use of the information contained within this document, including - but not limited to - errors, omissions, or inaccuracies.

Copyright © 2024 by J Craig and Clifford Marketing.
All rights reserved worldwide.

www.ingramcontent.com/pod-product-compliance
Lightning Source LLC
Chambersburg PA
CBHW072258310526
45795CB00012B/1822

* 9 7 9 8 8 7 9 9 7 5 5 7 4 *